The Library of
Turtles and Tortoises™

Snapping Turtles

Christopher Blomquist

The Rosen Publishing Group's
PowerKids Press™
New York

For Carolyn, a friend to kith and creatures

Published in 2004 by The Rosen Publishing Group, Inc.
29 East 21st Street, New York, NY 10010

First Edition

Editor: Natashya Wilson
Book Design: Michael J. Caroleo

Photo Credits: Cover, title page, pp. 7, 8, 16 by Bill Beatty; p. 4 © Joe McDonald/Animals Animals; p. 11 © DANI/JESKE/ Animals Animals; p. 12 © Breck P. Kent/Animals Animals; pp. 15, 19 © E. R. Degginger/Animals Animals; p. 20 © Leonard Lee Rue III/Animals Animals.

Blomquist, Christopher.
Snapping turtles / Christopher Blomquist.— 1st ed.
     v. cm. — (The Library of turtles and tortoises)
Includes bibliographical references (p.   ).
Contents: The big, bad biter — Reptiles and terrapins — Common snapping turtles — Alligator snapping turtles — Feeding time — Sleep tight — How snapping turtles multiply — Growing babies — Soups, stews, and other dangers.
ISBN 0-8239-6736-0 (lib. bdg.)
1. Snapping turtles—Juvenile literature. [1. Snapping turtles. 2. Turtles.] I. Title. II. Series.
QL666.C539 B58 2004
597.92'2—dc21

2002153314

Manufactured in the United States of America

Contents

The Big, Bad Biter

Just below the surface of the water, two eyes and a nose poke out from the muddy bottom of a lake, a stream, or a pond. The animal's face is hard to see because it is almost the same color as the dark water. Suddenly the creature's strong jaws snap down to catch another animal. The underwater **predator** called the snapping turtle has struck again!

Snapping turtles are well named. When they bite, their powerful jaws come together quickly in a loud snap. Snapping turtles are not gentle animals. In fact, these turtles are known for being mean. Although they usually avoid people, they will bite if they cannot move away or if they mistake a human limb for their usual food. Their bite is strong enough to cut right through a person's hand or foot!

Although snapping turtles come onto land once in a while, they usually stay in the water, swimming or resting on the bottom.

5

Reptiles and Terrapins

Snapping turtles and all other turtles are part of a group of animals called **reptiles**. Reptiles, which include animals such as crocodiles, lizards, and snakes, have several things in common. Most reptiles lay eggs on land and have bodies that are covered in hard scales. Reptiles also continue to grow throughout their lives. The older they get, the bigger they get! Snapping turtles, or snappers, are called **aquatic** turtles because they live mostly in the water. Aquatic, hard-shelled turtles are also called **terrapins**. Snappers live in freshwater or in **brackish** water, but not in the ocean. Aquatic turtles and all reptiles use lungs, not gills, to breathe, so snappers come up from the water for air. Snappers can stay underwater without taking a breath for at least 50 minutes.

Snapping turtles are often found in shallow, slow-moving water. Some will dive to depths of 10 feet (3 m).

Turtle and Tortoise Facts

People often call turtles that live only on dry land "tortoises." Snapping turtles are not called tortoises for one very simple reason. They spend most of their time in the water.

This map shows where snapping turtles live in North America. Their range stretches from southern Canada to the southern United States, mostly east of the Rocky Mountains.

Common Snapping Turtles

There are two different types, or **species**, of snapping turtles, the common and the alligator snapping turtles. The common snapping turtle is seen more often. It lives in parts of North America, Central America, and South America.

The top of a turtle's shell is called the **carapace**. A common snapper's carapace can be tan, brown, olive, or black. It can be up to 19 inches (48.2 cm) long. The carapace has pointy knobs on it that smooth out as the common snapper ages. The back of the carapace is **serrated**, or pointy edged. The common snapper's tail is about as long as its shell and is also serrated. The **plastron**, or bottom part of a turtle's shell, is much smaller on a common snapper than it is on most other types of turtles. It is shaped like a cross and is usually yellow or tan.

This is a common snapping turtle. Adult common snapping turtles weigh from 35 to 45 pounds (15.9–20.4 kg).

9

Alligator Snapping Turtles

The alligator snapping turtle is the largest freshwater turtle in North America. It can grow to weigh more than 200 pounds (90.7 kg). Alligator snappers have long tails, and their brown or green carapaces have three rows of bony points along the top, as an alligator's back has. This scary-looking turtle also has a large head, a set of four strong legs with clawed toes, and powerful, hook-shaped jaws. An adult alligator snapper's shell is usually between 16 and 31 inches (40.6–78.7 cm) long. The alligator snapper lives in the southern United States. It eats only fish. To catch them it uses a pink piece of flesh that sticks out from its tongue! This pink flesh looks like a wiggly worm. The turtle sits underwater with its mouth open and waits for a fish to take a nibble. Then it snaps down on the fish.

The pink, wormlike flesh can be seen on the bottom of this alligator snapper's mouth. Its jaws look like a bird's beak.

Turtle and Tortoise Facts

Turtles have been around for more than 200 million years. That's longer than any other type of reptile seen today!

Feeding Time

Unlike the alligator snapping turtle, the common snapping turtle eats more than fish. Common snappers are **omnivores**, which means they eat both animals and plants. Plants and **algae** make up about 36 percent of this turtle's diet. Its other favorite foods include bugs, frogs, salamanders, and sometimes even small waterbirds and turtles. It will eat any **prey** that it can swallow. The common snapper will also eat **carrion**, or the flesh of a dead animal. The turtle's strong sense of smell helps it to find dead animals under water. Like all turtles, snapping turtles do not have teeth. Instead they use their sharp jaws and claws to tear apart their food. Although snappers do not eat humans, they will bite humans from time to time. It is always best to keep your distance from a snapping turtle!

Snappers often hunt in places where they can hide, such as in reeds. This common snapper has caught a sunfish for its meal.

Sleep Tight

Snapping turtles are mostly **nocturnal** animals. This means that most of their activities, such as eating and swimming, take place at night. During the day, these turtles often rest in mud or float in shallow water. They blend with their surroundings and look just like rocks.

In the warm months when snappers are active, they live alone. However, snappers that live in places with cold winters may **hibernate** until the weather gets warmer. Some hibernate in groups, often stacking up on top of one another. They go to sleep for the winter in the banks and bottoms of streams or lakes, in deserted animal dens, or under logs and dead plants.

However, a few strong snappers stay active in the cold. They have been seen moving below the surface of ice-covered lakes and streams!

This common snapper lives in a swamp in New Jersey. Its brown color helps it to hide in the mud.

Turtle and Tortoise Facts

Many hibernating snapping turtles do not breathe. They bury themselves in the mud of a body of water that does not freeze at the bottom and get air from the water through the skin on their mouths and throats.

How Snapping Turtles Multiply

Snapping turtles **mate** in the water usually during the spring, and sometimes in the summer and the fall. Females may lay their eggs about one month after mating or may wait up to several years to lay their eggs. Most female snapping turtles lay from 20 to 40 eggs sometime in May or June. The eggs are white and have leathery shells. They are about the size of table-tennis balls. Common snapper eggs are smaller than alligator snapper eggs, which are about 1 ½ inches (3.8 cm) wide. Usually a female digs her nest near the water, in damp sand or dirt. She may also make a nest in a deserted animal den that is near the water. Once the female lays her eggs, she buries them. Then she leaves them and does not come back. When the baby turtles hatch, they must take care of themselves.

Female snappers use only their hind legs to dig their nests and then to position the eggs in the nest. They do this without looking.

Growing Babies

Common snapping turtle eggs take from 55 to 125 days to hatch. Alligator snapping turtle eggs take from 100 to 140 days. The nest must be slightly moist and must stay at a **temperature** of 68°F to 88°F (20°C–31.1°C) for the babies inside the eggs to grow. The warmer the nest, the faster the eggs will hatch. The nest's temperature **determines** whether male or female turtles are born. Temperatures between 69.8°F and 73.4°F (21°C–22°C) produce equal numbers of males and females. Cooler temperatures and temperatures above 82.4°F (29°C) produce mosly females. Newborn snappers' shells are from about 1 to 1 ½ inches (2.5–3.8 cm) long. Common snappers take from 4 to 19 years to become adults. Alligator snappers take from 11 to 13 years.

Hatchlings have a special egg tooth that helps them to break out of the egg. They shed this tooth about three weeks later.

Turtle and Tortoise Facts

Turtles' shells are made of bones that are covered by hard plates called scutes. The shell grows with the turtle. Young turtles' shells show growth rings, like those of trees.

Soups, Stews, and Other Dangers

Many snapping turtle eggs and babies are eaten by predators such as skunks, foxes, and raccoons. Only about 1 in 1,400 eggs laid will become an adult snapper. Animals that eat adult snappers include alligators, bears, coyotes, and humans. For hundreds of years, people have hunted snapping turtles for food. Snapping turtle meat is used to make tasty soups. People also eat the eggs. The eggs must be fried, for they will not hard-boil.

Unlike many turtle species, snapping turtles cannot pull their heads completely into their shells to protect themselves from danger. However, thanks to these turtles' strong bite and hard shell, they are fairly well protected. Scared or angry snappers give off a bad smell from **glands** near their tail. They will also hiss to drive away enemies.

This skunk is feasting on a nest of snapping turtle eggs. Most eggs that get eaten are found within 24 hours of being laid.

21

Born to Be Wild

Healthy common snapping turtles will usually live for 30 to 40 years. Alligator snappers may live for 70 years or more. Snappers do not make good pets! They grow too big and are unsafe to touch. Some turtle fans do keep snappers as pets, but most say that caring for them is neither fun nor easy. Snapping turtles are best left in the wild where they belong. If you do not get too close to a snapping turtle, it probably will not bother you. These turtles usually attack only when they've been pulled from the water onto dry land. That really makes them mad! These special creatures help to keep nature in balance. They keep the animals they eat from becoming too numerous, and they are food for other animals. If you come across a snapper, keep your distance and let this special snapping animal go about its life.

Glossary

algae (AL-jee) A plantlike living thing without roots or stems that lives in water.

aquatic (uh-KWAH-tik) Living or growing in water, not on land.

brackish (BRA-kish) Somewhat salty.

carapace (KER-uh-pays) The upper part of a turtle's shell.

carrion (KAR-ee-un) Dead, rotting flesh.

determines (dih-TER-minz) Decides.

glands (GLANDZ) Organs or parts of the body that produce an element to help with a bodily function.

hibernate (HY-bur-nayt) To spend the winter in a sleeplike state.

mate (MAYT) To join together to make babies.

nocturnal (nok-TUR-nul) Active during the night.

omnivores (OM-nih-vorz) Animals that eat both plants and animals.

plastron (PLAS-tron) The bottom, flatter part of a turtle's shell that covers the belly.

predator (PREH-duh-ter) An animal that kills other animals for food.

prey (PRAY) An animal that is hunted by another animal for food.

reptiles (REP-tylz) A group of cold-blooded animals with lungs and scales, such as turtles, snakes, and lizards.

serrated (ser-AYT-ed) Having toothlike points at the end.

species (SPEE-sheez) A single kind of plant or animal. All humans are one species.

temperature (TEM-pruh-chur) How hot or cold something is.

terrapins (TER-uh-pinz) Hard-shelled turtles that live mostly in water.

Index

Web Sites

Due to the changing nature of Internet links, PowerKids Press has developed an online list of Web sites related to the subject of this book. This site is updated regularly. Please use this link to access the list:
www.powerkidslinks.com/ltt/snapping/